FOXES

by Michelle Levine

PULL AHEAD BOOKS
Animals

Lerner Publications Company • Minneapolis

This book is available in two editions:
Library binding by Lerner Publications Company, a division of Lerner Publishing Group, Inc.
Soft cover by First Avenue Editions, an imprint of Lerner Publishing Group, Inc.
241 First Avenue North
Minneapolis, MN 55401 U.S.A.

Website address: www.lernerbooks.com

Words in *italic* type are explained in a glossary on page 30.

Library of Congress Cataloging-in-Publication Data

Michelle Levine.
    Red foxes / by Michelle Levine.
      p.   cm. — (Pull ahead books)
    Summary: An introduction to the physical characteristics,
  behavior, and habitat of the red fox.
    ISBN-13: 978-0-8225-3774-8 (lib. bdg. : alk. paper)
    ISBN-10: 0-8225-3774-5 (lib. bdg. : alk. paper)
    ISBN-13: 978-0-8225-9887-9 (pbk. : alk. paper)
    ISBN-10: 0-8225-9887-6 (pbk. : alk. paper)
    1. Red fox—Juvenile literature. [1. Red fox. 2. Foxes.] I. Title. II. Series.
  QL737.C22W38 2004
  599.775—dc22   2003016546

Manufactured in the United States of America
2 3 4 5 6 7 — JR — 12 11 10 09 08 07

Zoom! An animal is running fast.

What animal is it?

This animal
is a red fox.

Foxes are *mammals*.

All mammals have hair or fur.
Most red foxes have red fur.

White fur
covers the
underside
of a red fox.

The tip of a red fox's tail
is white, too.

A fox's tail is big and bushy.
It keeps a sleeping fox warm.

When do foxes sleep?

Foxes sleep during the day
most of the time.

Foxes are *nocturnal*. They are active at night.

Foxes usually look for food at night.

Foxes are *omnivores.*

They eat both plants and animals.

Red foxes hunt mice, rabbits, and other small animals.

Hunted animals are called *prey.*

Sniff. Sniff. A hunting fox smells prey nearby.

The fox uses its pointy ears
to listen for the prey.

It uses its sharp eyes to find the prey.

This fox is chasing its prey.
Foxes can run for a long time.

How else does a fox catch its prey?

Sometimes a fox *stalks* its prey.

A stalking fox moves slowly
and quietly.

Surprise! The stalking fox pounces on its prey.

The fox catches the prey
with its claws.

It eats the prey with its sharp teeth.

A fox buries any extra food
under the ground.

Later, the fox will dig up the food
and eat it.

Is this fox digging for food?

No. It is digging a *den*.
A fox family lives in a den.

Some foxes dig their own dens.

Many foxes live in the empty dens
of other animals.

Baby foxes are born in a den.

Baby foxes are called *kits*.

These kits are one month old.

They are ready to explore.

The young foxes stay near
their den at first.

They play and fight.

Then they learn to stalk and hunt.

A red fox sets out on its own after about six months.

This red fox is all grown up!

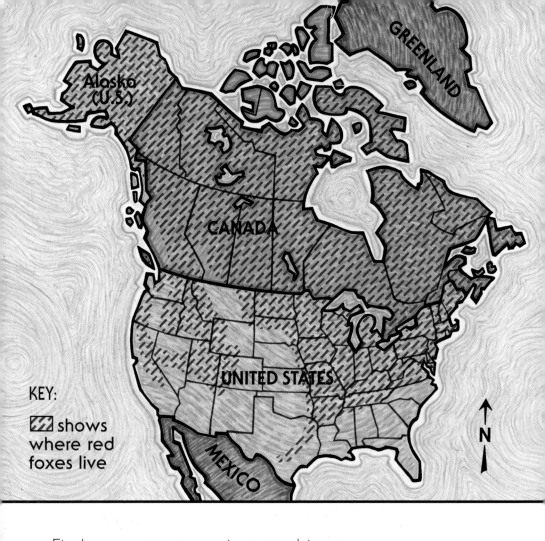

KEY:

▨ shows where red foxes live

Find your state or province on this map.
Do red foxes live near you?

Parts of a Red Fox's Body

ear

head

eye

fur

nose

mouth

tail

front leg

back leg

paw

claw

Glossary

den: a safe place under the ground where a fox family lives

kits: baby foxes

mammals: an animal that has hair or fur and drinks its mother's milk when it is young

nocturnal: animals that are active at night

omnivores: animals that eat both plants and animals

prey: animals that are hunted by other animals

stalks: sneaks up on a hunted animal. A stalking fox moves slowly and quietly.

Hunt and Find

- a fox **catching** its prey on pages 15–17
- a fox **eating** on pages 11, 18
- a fox **running** on pages 3, 15
- a fox **digging** its den on pages 20–21
- fox **kits** on pages 22–25
- a **sleeping** fox on pages 8–9

About the Author

Michelle Levine is a writer and editor living in St. Paul, Minnesota.

Photo Acknowledgments

The photos in this book are reproduced with the permission of: © Michele Burgess, front cover, p. 5; © Joe McDonald/Visuals Unlimited, pp. 3, 18, 20; PhotoDisc, pp. 4, 12, 26; © Alan and Sandy Carey, pp. 6, 9, 17, 23, 27; © Gary W. Carter/Visuals Unlimited, pp. 7, 31; © G. VandeLeest/Visuals Unlimited, p. 8; © Rob & Ann Simpson/Visuals Unlimited, p. 10; © Ernest Manewal/Visuals Unlimited, p. 11; © Glenn Oliver/Visuals Unlimited, p. 13; © Arthur Morris/Visuals Unlimited, p. 14; © Gerard Fuehrer/Visuals Unlimited, p. 15; © Jack Ballard/Visuals Unlimited, p. 16; © Ron Spomer/Visuals Unlimited, p. 19; © Will Troyer/Visuals Unlimited, pp. 21, 25; © Wilford Miller/Visuals Unlimited, p. 22; © Adam Jones/Visuals Unlimited, p. 24.